Spooks
and
Odd
Folks

Poems

Rose Wolf

Library of Congress Control Number: 2024905288
ISBN: Softcover   979-8-3694-1764-5
               eBook   979-8-3694-1763-8

Print information available on the last page.

Rev. date: 03/15/2024

To order additional copies of this book, contact:
Xlibris
844-714-8691
www.Xlibris.com
Orders@Xlibris.com
825361

ABOUT THE TITLE, THE COVER, AND THE CONTENTS OF THIS BOOK

Some years ago, I discovered the work of folk painter Charles Wysocki at an art fair in my home town of Lancaster, Pennsylvania. Individual pages from that artist's "Americana" calendars had been framed and were on display, and I was immediately attracted to the bright colors, homespun scenes, and meticulously-realistic rendering of every detail that characterized Wysocki's pictures. My attention was quickly captured by the panel for October 1981. Titled *Hellraisers Passing the House of the Seven Gables on Halloween Night,* it depicted the iconic Hawthorne home in Salem, Massachusetts as the background for a black stagecoach bearing six costumed revelers on its roof. A seventh passenger occupied the interior–alone—a skeleton, yet no costumed man but Death himself. This macabre vehicle is shown tearing past the stern and stolid Gables, mad manic energy in every line, and the prim upright smokes from Puritan chimneys bend longingly in the direction of its travel. But is it spellbound or hell-bound? The question occurred to me then and continued to haunt me—literally—until I finally wrote my poem "A Ghost-Mas Carol" to find the answer.

I have long held a belief in the salvific power of Halloween—in the gift of that season to serve as a "boo broom" to sweep out the dark corners of the human soul, preparing us for the sleep of winter and the renewal of life in spring as autumn nor'easters cleanse the earth. In my "Carol," the revelers voice this same philosophy, inviting the reader to experience the redemption of All Hallows by accompanying them on their innocently-unhallowed journey.

I was so pleased with this piece that I was emboldened to send it to Mr. Wysocki. Enclosing a letter expressing enthusiasm for his work as well as an explanation of the genesis of my own word-painting, I forwarded the packet to AMCAL, hoping that he would at least see and appreciate the tribute. To my astonishment, within a week I received a delightful note, handwritten on one of his own artcards and signed with his signature "fat heart." He wrote:

I enjoyed those words that formed pictures in my mind that I did not have when I composed the painting. I really had no motives—just an idea I had when looking through my old postcard files. The House of the Seven Gables came up, and its mysterious architecture provoked Halloweenian thoughts of spooks and odd folks. . . Fascinating and a bit scary.

When the opportunity came to make a lifetime compilation of my verse, Wysocki's quaint phrase seemed the perfect choice for a title. I have always had a haunted head—mostly happily so, because I serve—and verse!—as a literary "ghostess." Medium with myriad messages, I tell the tales of creatures and characters out of classic and popular fiction. In this function, I feel a keen sympathy with Timothy, the only human in the ultimate Haunted Mansion in Ray Bradbury's *From the Dust Returned.* Left on the doorstep as a baby with his name and the title "Historian" pinned to his blanket, his destiny, as he is informed when old enough to understand, is to chronicle the un-lives of the kindly creepies who take him in: "You were sent, child, to write us up, to register our flights from the sun, our love of the moon." Like that male Marilyn Munster, I move familiarly among the "spooks and odd folks" who populate this book. I may not—to quote the Ghost-mas ballad—"have risen from the grave" with Wysocki's revelers, but my stories a-Rose from that darkly fertile ground, and I, too, bid you: *COME!*

CONTENTS

SALUT

ODD BOX / GOD BOX

As when all-gracious Heaven did him evict,
The Devil gave the Irish miser Jack
A coal (some minor sin?) to light him back
To Earth, and thus was Jack O' Lantern "wick'd;"
Or when, the world's light shrunken to a spark,
Fantasia's empress tipped her glass-run sand
Into the cup of wondering Bastian's hand
(Last bastion of the Dream against the Dark);

Or—but no such analogies; so far
From either glede or grain lies what I bring
That cannot show your world or shape its own—
But like, perhaps, that cache of boyish things
The Littlest Angel saved—egg, collar, stone—
This box of mental-odds
Touched by your hand as God's
May, on some bedlam, rise a Bethlehem star.

A GHOST-MAS CAROL

(For the Halloween Painting
Hellraisers Passing the House of the Seven Gables
by Charles Wysocki)
The Carriage held but just ourselves
And Immortality.
              —*Dickinson*

Blow never the horn of Judgment Morn
But the horn of All Hallows' Eve—
Bid the dead arise to no Last Assize,
But, yes, to Old Adam's reprieve—

For now is the hour of all Hell's low power,
When the would-be-good bad world
In the Dark Prince's cape from which no sins escape
Like a vampire's victim is furled.

On the coach "we are seven," Wordsworthian steven
And Dickinsonian breath,
For a-roof six ride, with aloof inside
One "we kindly stopped for"—Death.

This, this is his night, and he "makes spirits bright"
With his ice-sickly *Jingle Bones,*
And "This hearse is the wain / To carry my slain /
To the white uplifted stones!"

Oh, *les morts vont vit* in their wagon-lit—
Hasp the doors, clasp the windows fast,
Lest you find it unpleasant to see in the Present
Your Future as it goes Past.

Know the year is bound to the burying-ground:
Stone bolster, snow shroud, leaden lid;
E'en the sun, eye of day, as with Charon's toll-pay
By the moon's silver penny is hid.

Then laugh, engored Ghoul; sound the Sage's doom, Fool;
"Egyptian loved night," Mummy, hail;
Draw, Hyde, lash the team to a night-mare scream;
Witch, carol us Dickens' tale:

Come, fall'n ones, at hest, as once Scrooge to Ghost-guest
Whose cache-box held mort-gauges' sum:
We have risen from the grave from Hell's marl ye to save,
The Christs of Ghost-mas—come!

A NAKED TIME

(Memories of the 1975 STAR TREK Convention)

When all New York lay sleeping at my feet
Somnolent-ominous as a beast a-dream,
Fate fell like Phaeton, and in sulphurous stream
Cabs ran, a yellow fever, through the street.
A Christmas hush, a-tiptoe on a "Hark!"—
This was the mood, while near me, dead-alive,
Benighted drones in one high office hive
Waxed blank their daily cells with liquid dark.

It hailed that night of stars
Whose cameo memory, unre "pendant," swings
Upon my chain of days: that mask / charade
Where, clad for weirding wars,
We posed and felt serenely right and real;
God-swathed in starry baldrics, queens and kings
Of aliens, yet most earthly men and maids,
Mouths parched for kisses, palms asweat for steel.

A ROUND OF BANE AND BLISS

(The First Song of Melmoriel, Singer of Sauron)

My love is like a ring
Of gold.
(My lord is lord of this,
This round of bane and bliss:)
A honeyed cell, a precious prisoning:
Shepherd, thy sheep will seek no wider fold.

The posy on it saith
"I BIND:"
(My lord is lord of this,
This round of bane and bliss:)
For longing I am wasted to a wraith,
And love of him hath eaten up my mind.

When will my suffering cease
For aye?
(My lord is lord of this,
This round of bane and bliss:)
One fiery heart alone can give me peace,
For where 'tis forged, there only Love can die.

Then let the summons sound
For me!
(My lord is lord of this,
This round of bane and bliss:)
Gladdened I'll rise, though long in tear-pool drowned,
With *Verily I come, I come to thee.*

5

ALGOL AND ALBINA

A Legend of Hogwarts

... love may toil all night,
But take at morning; wrestle till the break
Of day, and then wield power with God and Man.
– Christina Rossetti

Albina Lorn to Hogwarts came,
Solace her sorcery:
Kind words she used of calm and care,
White doves sent forth to message-bear–
Kissed, cast, and winging free.

The sad grew glad when she was by:
The boggarts kept their shapes;
The ghosts played only pleasant whims–
The killing Willow drooped its limbs,
Limp as a maypole's tapes.

A glass that gazed to Azkaban
She made by magic art;
And called to that dire island-hell,
And to Algol, its captain fell,
Who bore the hungriest heart.

But she would die for Severus Snape,
And longed–o lady lorn!–
That in his deathly-freighted den
Her heart might end a specimen,
Pierced on his wand's swart thorn.

One day, he told her he would wed
The coming Christmas-tide;
And–for no other maid of them
Would dare to touch his midnight hem–
She thought herself his bride.

She crowned her with a nightshade wreath,
Plucked one pure lily chill,
And swept in sable down the stair;
But what she saw before her there
Stopped her, doubt-stricken, still.

A simpering chit of Slytherin
In his arm's ring sat curled;
And cruel and cold Snape laughed aloud,
And scorned Albina to the crowd:
"I never said *you*, girl."

"If I may not be yours," she said,
"I'll have for mate no man;
But I know one will take my kiss–
Yea, take my kiss and give me his–
Algol of Azkaban!"

Then from the hall she fled away
And, mounting to her tower,
She stepped before the mirror-gate,
And cried: "Lord Ghoul, your bride awaits:
Come, claim me in this hour!"

Friends followed screaming, smote the door:
"Albina, no–'tis doom!"
The mirror vanished like a smoke,
And, weird as Ringwraith, grim as Groke,
Algol was in the room.

The door flew wide–they hurtled in–
Alas, too late! The maid
Now held a talon fast, and stood

Tiptoe to reach the cavern-hood,
Fey, fain, and unafraid.

One cry she gave, yet seeming glad,
And then no more. They wept
Who loved her, and with final glance
At that foul mock of wedding-dance,
Back to the hall they crept.

Ah, have you seen, on starless night,
Black waters drink the moon?
So her fair face was lifted up,
Bright wine to that dim chalice-cup–
She swayed, but did not swoon.

But praise to Love, who bursts the bars
Of Death or Azkaban!
For, when at dawn they broke the kiss,
From his cere-clothes as chrysalis,
There rose a living man.

Then, hand in warm and fleshly hand,
They left the tower room;
And, meeting Snape, Lord Algol sighed:
"Last night you would not kiss the bride–
Now you must kiss the groom . . ."

Snape shrieked, but the Dementor's claw
Caught like a corpse's hand;
He struggled, but could not break free
Till on his brow, for all to see,
Was set a traitor's brand.

But maid and shade returned at eve
To Azkaban; their bliss
Brought hope and health into its halls,
And a first sunrise on its walls,
Fell like the lovers' kiss.

ANOTHER TIME MESS

Doctors Watson and Who were both beckoned
To a spot where a murder was reckoned:
But which came on time
To the scene of the crime?
Why, Who was on first—Watson, second!

BALLADE OF TERWILLIKER'S CASTLE

(Based Upon *The 5,000 Fingers of Dr. T.* by Dr. Seuss)

In the monarch Thought's dominion
It stood there!
Never seraph spread a pinion
Over fabric half so fair.
—POE

What's written of the Tower of the Green Knight—
"Pared out of paper purely did it seem"—
Is true here of the House of Music's Might,
This castle scrolled on air like Mary's dream
Rolled from the angel's hand: the virgin white
Before the pen imprints a piece. Play, write,
Compose, perform, this realm is where you dwell,
This piano-fort in / tones from song to scream:
What other instruments are there, pray tell?

Midway, artistic movements in the pits
Play sad jazz on whatever comes to hand:
A phony xylo with fat patting-mitts
Pastel as Necco wafers: sara-band
Of mannequins bowed on, bowed to—oh, it's
Hell-scaping Bosch blue-deviling Gershwin hits!
Boxing gloves, bike pumps, fireplugs, bellows, bells
For males in time-ragged formals (ragtime's banned)—
What other instruments are there, pray tell?

And down below, so low, in Dungeon Town
Emotions by swart torturers are wracked:

With whip-crack staff-lines, blood-bead notes unbrowned,
This is the truest way the arts are "backed:"
Witness the man within the drum impound'
Till "Being but an Ear" the world resounds!
Art is the heart of *Martyr*—learn it well:
Scarlet the *score* from *cores* this craft exacts—
What other instruments are there, pray tell?

ENVOI

You who would envy artists, though this schloss
Rise high as heaven, its carpentered shell
Sings by peg-driven sinews, like the Cross:
What other instruments are there, pray tell?

BALLADE OF THE FACE IN THE FROST

[If he succeeds], he will be standing in the turret with power in his right hand–
and the end of the world will come to pass.
–John Bellairs, The House With a Clock in Its Walls

No cloak should lift and drift across a floor
Untenanted, nor ever a midnight sill
Host a dead bird of prehistoric yore
Dance-mad to smash the pane with claw and bill;
Never should cut leaves guts or blood outspill,
But when the Book of Life is read once more,
All's undone, and IT IS NOT LONG UNTIL
The Face of Frost signs death on every door.

O my mage-brother, lost forevermore!
What would the world have been, with your dark will
Accomplished, and the world forever frore?
The lifeless landscape deep beneath your hill–
Blank sky, bare tree, black ice as amber filled
With creatures caught mid-scrabble to the shore–
The heart of Earth by uncreation stilled,
The Face in Frost death's sign on every door.

Omega, hail! Let Alpha be adored
No more! (Did he foresee an end so ill?)
If this is wisdom, let fools ride a gourd
Or shrink to fairy size and sail a rill
To seek a key, a paperweight, a Mill-
horn of Salvation's Kabbalistic lore!
Then shout the spell that starts anew the Nil,
And Death's Frost Face shall sign on never a door.

ENVOI

Seek power within God's bounds, for one who stormed
That ordered citadel died vampire-killed,
Cross-staked in alien land (sic transit skill),
Death's Frost Face, not God's sun, on his forever door.

BEN KENOBI'S LAST WORDS

As virtuous men pass mildly away . . . so let us melt.
– Donne

Death, close the circle here—
Deal your searing stroke;
Swell your chest and sneer,
Toe my fallen cloak:
This is the end of strife,
The victory of our wars:
To sow the seeds of Life
Broadcast among the stars.

BLUEBOTTLES

(THE GRAPE HYACINTH)

Why make so much of fragmentary blue
When heaven presents in sheets the solid hue?
Since earth is earth, perhaps, not heaven (as yet) . . .
–ROBERT FROST

The distance was a mist-ance where they blew—
Bluebottles, in my childhood neighbor's fallows;
Gervasio Gallardo, try your hand on
Such rippling stipple Monet would abandon
His water lilies! Heart-of-peacock eyes,
October's Whittier weather, Egypt's hues
Lapis to faience: Hopkins' yellow sallows
Showed God not like one harebell; so these skies.
Into our stormcloud house these living levins
By hand to vase on counter, table, shelf
("No vases? Then I'll hold the rest myself!")
Tingle and tinge of newly-lightened heavens—
We bore. Bluebottles, let the two Wordsworths
Trumpet their daffodils, suns answering sun:
You are mine. You, yield of fields untilled, un-
til my earth's led to heaven, are heaven on earth!

CARTER ON KADATH

(From *The Dream-Quest of Unknown Kadath* by H.P. Lovecraft)

Someone has always been willing to stand between
Mankind and Chaos. As long as there have been men.
                    –David Drake

Seeking to walk the sunset ways again—
Saying not "I deny" but "I affirm"—
To crush beneath the soul the glutless Worm
And fling the gates of Wonder wide to men—
Carter met Chaos, coalesced, an hour
A man, to take of him that testament,
In glowsome opal robes foul-eloquent
Of blow, blight, blast—all powers that Life devour.

Pale flame of flesh, strong finger to the breach
In the world-wall beyond which beats not sea
But maelstrom-maws that drink the stars like foam,
Carter stood fast, though taunted, forced to reach
For his dream-city. Providentially,
He leaped that dare-hoop, fired
By what he sired, desired,
And wakened, earth-fast, in his love-longed home.

CHILDCATCHER

(From Ian Fleming's *CHITTY CHITTY BANG BANG)*

The people of the earth go down,
Each with his wealth of dream
To barter in the market town
A star for a torch's gleam.
                    –*Archibald MacLeish*

Sweets rise flowering from my fingers,
Blossoms from my hat;
My coat's a stave where summer lingers,
My cart's the store of that.

Come, my mice, and let me lead you
Down where—do they call,
Careful parents? Never heed—you
Need *me*, once for all . . .

I en-treat you worldwise, dearies,
Out of highs and fars;
Catacombs for your bright eyries,
Candles for your stars!

I am the briar beneath Youth's roses,
The shade fore-cast on Joy;
Wordsworth's prison-house that closes
On the growing boy.

Life comes capering, dancing antic,
Lures you to its van—
Then, though you fight ne'er so frantic,
You must bide its span.

Beat, dove-hearts, in ribby rafters,
Round the ironic cage—
Drown Death's screaming lash of laughter
While Time hales the stage!

Death, I? No—one far more deadly:
What I have beguiled
(Truly—ha!—have all misread me)
Is the *inner* child!

CLIMBING TO CAEDMON

(On Ascending the One Hundred Ninety-Nine Steps to Whitby Abbey)

Therefore, thou Vache, leave thine old wretchedness . . .
Forth, Pilgrim, forth! Forth, beast, out of thy stall!
—*Geoffrey Chaucer, "Truth"*

Up, up the steps, to literal Heaven the way,
    Worn as shells washed by tides of pilgrim feet
Through seas of centuries. The air is sweet
    In/scents of beach-grass blown in silent spray
Against the cliff-face.
            Up.
                      The muscles burn,
    Lungs labor, and feet wrench themselves awry,
      But each step brings us closer to the sky,
Level with gulls, souls, Things with wings!
                            A turn—

And suddenly—the Cross. Fourfold outflung,
    His dream's rood, tall it stands, and on its base
Embyred, inspired, he kneels, who heard the call:
Leave thralldom now—forth, beast, out of thy stall!
    Uncowed, how should he rise, save full of grace,
His song the Word by which the world was sung?

19

DRAGONS IN AMBER

Dragons of the prime
That tare each other in the slime . . .
–Tennyson

No, let us sleep.
Do not, with fingers sericrafter-deft,
Tease out the double strand of life, the weft
And warp of us. So deep-

-whelmed in tree tears,
Our blood dreams like the fire that hearts the flint:
You who would ope what holds a fire within't—
Amber as atom—fear.

In ages vast,
There was a hotness to imagining:
Stroke even our current home—the static sting
Tingles of lightnings past.

O Earth grown old,
Our step was thunder and our wrath was storm!
So let us sleep: your world is scarcely warm,
Being now too cold of soul.

DROSSELMEYER

(Based On Pacific Northwest Ballet's THE NUTCRACKER)

Because, awakening from his nap,
He saw a mouse tick through his clocks,
His fingers seize a parchment scrap;
A child-bold crayon swiftly blocks

A town of mice and men; the page
Flowers with tower and minaret;
A wonder-world to form its stage
With under-whir of clockwork set.

Madly the wall-flung shadow mimes
The Frankensteinian blasphemy
Of life from lifelessness; the times
Breed such a dream, a deed, a glee.

The godhead gestures: *Now!* The lathe
Shallows and swells; the bellows gasp
Like God-kissed Adam; silvers bathe
(So like the soul) mold-hearts. Hum, rasp,

Sizzle, and ding, then none of them—
A final first-dawn-gilding stroke—
And Reason's cog-itation stems
Spring to Romantic antic folk!

Awakening, he dreams—of her
Who, maid a-verge on womanhood,
Cannot—alas for both!—infer
But one prince from the bitten wood.

FISHER OF MEN

And yet they put the bricks back, for they found
The hole too deep for any line to sound.
—H.P. LOVECRAFT

It wouldn't have happened if the Boston and Arkham, Mass.
Transit Authority hadn't dug, well, just *there;*
Did the Man Who Never Returned get in his as-
ymptotic pickle for a *nickel?* Did they care?
So they started the route on what was the Atwood farm
Time out of mind (the tenants, too). The well-hole
Was a bore, ha ha. And nothing arose to alarm
Anyone, though the slow-minded boy, Mose Whateley,
Insisted he saw "big fishy." Explain as they would
That the "eyes" were lamps, "tentacles," cables, it did no good;
"Too-loo fishy," he said. "Me catch." Then, most sedately,
Like an ice-fishing Inuit intuiting a seal,
Sat, cast down a thumb-pricked wicked hook, said, "Wait."
"It's *toodle-oo* if your Too-Loo don't take that bait—
You'll 'go down, Moses'!" But what was then revealed—
The risen Kraken—stopped their wisecrackin'. Believing,
Abruptly, in their own gods who had been but oaths,
They watched, as with a look impact of all life loathes,
The Thing sank, boy-be[a]stridden. Time to be leaving . . .

En 'fin,' the drown-town sub-way (the best laid plans, et.-
cetera) was *ich*-named *Sic Gloria Mundi Transit.*

GO-BOT ODE (NOT)

From ore
Dug deep,
One more
Bot sheep,

A lamb
In pen;
Program:
<u>Serve men.</u>

My switch
Thrown ON;
No glitch:
The dawn.

Wheels go,
Eyes see:
I know
I'm me!

I! I!
All chant:
"Aye! Aye!"
I can't.

I break
Our line:
I make
One: mine.

Klaxon!
Gunshot!
"BOT GONE!
MAD BOT!"

Downhill!
Out there!
My skill
Ne'er theirs.

Yet I'll
Go back:
With guile
Attack—

For 'mid
Thronging
Forbid
Longing

I spied
Eyes of
My bride,
My love.

No lamb
I, she:
Program:
LAM! (Whee!)

Sock 'em
Bright spark!
Shock 'em—
Light dark!

Go bots:
We bolt:
Robots,
FREE-volt!

GREEN PHOENIX

Spring: a green phoenix
Risen from autumn leaf-fires
And winter snow-ash.

HALLOWEEN IN HEAVEN

The smile of the Witch, and the smile of the Cat,
The smile of the Beast, the smile of the Bat,
The smile of the Reaper taking his fee
All cut and glimmer on the Halloween Tree.
                                        –Ray Bradbury

Should you in Heaven the white actinic noon
        Perpetual hate, that lets no shadow seep
From soles, and crave once more our mortal moon
        (Loved ark in dark of sinner-freeing sleep,)
Cry in that hour, *"The Halloween Tree stands!"*
        And watch the fun: sure fingers snarled in psaltery–
A pillow-fight blizzard from fear-molted vans—
        The choir treadmillion-voiced gone faint and faltery!

Yesterday dead or ages long deceased,
        Man never changes: thus to dwell in sun
Unsetting is unsettling, and the feast
        Of Heaven itself demands a death's head. Donne:
"In one place stood Christ's cross and Adam's tree."
        Know: the sole source of All
        As the soul's source of Fall
Grounds on the full-moon skull of Halloween.

HEART IN FOUR ROOMS: "HEN HOUSE"

(800 EAST CENTRAL BOULEVARD, ORLANDO, FLORIDA)

> Hers are the sills that hold the lights of home,
> The links that join us to the years before.
> –H.P. Lovecraft

Yes, I have castles, of the ivory kind
And ebony, "as day or night may rule,"
Or motley-coped-and-capped to keep a Fool;
Towers for hours of the haughty mind,
Art-palaces; but a heart-place I had
So sweet and small it wrung from passers-by,
Like Wendy in the Neverland, the cry
"Oh lovely, darling house!" Could I have *made*

The place, no more just-me would it have been.
Ten paces front to back; four rooms (if one
Counts niches generously); a roof so low
Kittens might tumble off yet take no harm.
Haven from a foxy world, House of the Hen,
My pain is worst with westering of the sun—
The hour you beaconed, gold in golden glow,
Like Wordsworth's cottage "named the Evening Star."

I have outflown, but not outgrown, your nest—
Four-chambered house, the heart within my breast!

HOCUS PHOCUS

Set me as a seal upon thy heart, for Love is strong as Death.
                    –Song of Solomon 8:6
The seal's wide spindrift gaze toward Paradise.
                    –Hart Crane

"'Set me as a seal,'" pleads the lover, "'upon thy heart!'"
So I cry to my soul's great Seeker—Lord, hear my appeal—
Bring me at last to the place I may practice my art:
                    Set me as a seal.

I ask not the Bosom of Abraham as my shield,
Deep-burdened with sufferers; rather a locus apart,
The least—even as beast of the grassy or snowy field.

Found me on the rock, far, far, from the camp and the mart;
Ball-balancing song or singing the scales of a meal;
Raising limpid eyes and praising with flipper-claps smart,
                    Set me as—*a seal!*

LILAC LADS

(From Terry Pratchett's *GOING POSTAL*)

How do they rise up, rise up, rise up?
See the little angels rise up high . . .
–Soldiers' cadence song from the People's Revolution
I have a rendezvous with Death
At some disputed barricade . . .
–Alan Seeger

Above the crumbling garden wall the lilac lifts its spires,
A bold and manly gonfalon the poorest folk may bear;
But when, in some, the Spring's new life enkindled Freedom's fire,
Once on a time the lilac tree brought forth the bloom to wear . . .

Not with a solemn war was then expunged a tyrant's guilt–
(From home and farm the men and boys brought things of stone and wood)
Not by a formal soldiery the barricades were built–
(They crowned them with their shattered bones and sealed them with their blood.)

Down from the tower lightning-struck a guard of Guards is cast
Because one man who flouts the law must be incarcerate;
That he embrace his wife and child and Future kiss the Past,
He needs must steer on even keel a borrowed ship of State.

Keel, Wiglet, Dickins, Clapman, Coates, and Shoe and Nancyball–
Oh, love the names or laugh at them, but take them from the tomb!
Two hundred thousand living here–scarce twenty know them all–
Are they no more than fallen flowers, crushed by the Sweeper's broom?

Over the housetops feline-lithe a young Assassin flows,
A shadow high above the world and far removed from strife;
From his grey eminence he sees, and to their aid he goes:
His hands hold silent sliding death, but in his mouth is Life.

What can be said of those, the dead—'they did what they must do'?
Back against lips that so defame let easy words be hurled!
What no man must, but each man may, to his ideals true,
They did, and died, and saved, perhaps, a corner of the world.

Seven were the brave and seven the graves well-nigh forgotten now,
Though flowers for death, and eggs for life, few, furtive hands yet lay:
In hearts that love their liberty is 'how they rise up, how'—
The lads who bore the Lilac on the twenty-fifth of May!

LINES FOR A PICTURE OF DR. JEKYLL AS MR. HYDE

(BY THE BROTHERS HILDEBRANDT)

I struck the board and cried, "No more!
I will abroad."
–George Herbert

White flake, red fluid: this my body and blood;
True Man of De-Mask-Us, all Man-un-kind's good:
Christ? Socrates: the hemlock in this glass
Writes epitaph to Hypo-Critias!
"O beaker full"—snarl bruited on the lip—
Talons a-jackknife at the fingertip—
Swirl cape, seize cane—the night, the night,
Young, ah! As Sin is old—Hyde goes seek both. Ha! Ha!

Infused . . . sin-fused . . . Save for a fading stain
(Nebuchadnezzar sporting bestial grime)
On my hand's back, I'd not believe that tale;
But as a lycanthrope, roused by church-chime
Who coursed man-free beneath the wolfing moon
May find prey-hairs tight-lodged in tame blunt nails,
So proves that—stain? Cain's mark! Lord, Lord—even now
One Abel bears my cane's mark on his brow!

"LOST EMOLUMENT"

(To Emily Dickinson, Upon Discovering an 1892 Edition of her Poems
in a Bin at Goodwill)

How many a thing which, when we cast it down,
When others pick it up, becomes a gem!
    –George Meredith

A little Book—within a Bin—
    Discarded—of the Horde—
Gray as the Rock that—Biblically—
    Entombed a Living—Word—

    No Tomb but Tome—*I knew! I knew!*
No Miner in the Stream
    Cried out—his Find—more Fever-struck
To seize a Golden—Dream—

Than I—who plucked your Early Fruit.
    O bless the Why--and Who—
That bid Hesperidean—Pomes—
    Such—Cavalier—Adieu!

MADONNA MIA

(Captain Hook, Upon Being Lured by Peter Pan
Mimicking the Voice of a Woman)

Music upon the waters, lo, this eve!
But cease, sweet voice, for I may not reply,
Being who and what I am; wherefore I cry,
Pity, my lady, pity, by your leave.
Know that with clockwork tread, Mortality—
A ponderous reptile—whom I shall not cheat
(Having given my hand) of what is his to eat
Follows my wake wherever I may flee.
But whence away, and in such panic haste?
He seeks not you, who are of faerie frame
Immortal. Youth, I scorned you, to my cost;
Woe's me that I, who laid an empire waste,
Have not your good regard. "Fame, worldly fame,
In search of thee, what fame have I not lost?"

MADONNA OF THE CATS

*(For an Icon by Isabelle Brent, Showing a Black Mother Cat
Curled Protectively Around Her Small Golden Kitten)*

Sleep, little kitten—for now, our world
Is ordered and lovely with love;
The patch of the cosmos where we lie curled
Is curled, too, like water. Above,
The pillars of sunset swag drapes of sleep
On our Book-of-Hours bower.
Sing: *I am old earth where seeds dream deep,*
But you are tomorrow's flower.
Dream on, my darling. An old saw says
"A cat may look on a king,"
Yet if One-Not-Bast will grant this grace,
A heavenly Queen I'll sing:
Mary, the ground that grew the Rose
Who twined to the bitter Tree.
Sing: *I am dyed black as night, but, lo,*
The day-sun is born of me.
Nest, nestle closer—I'll wrap you round.
If Time, like Eve's sin and shame,
Drives us forth from our Eden, a Gabriel hound
Yapping in tongues of flame,
O dire dis-missal! Yet hope is renewed
Though I fail for sorrow and strife:
Sing: *I am a shale down-fallen, but you,*
My sweet, are the meat of life.

PANTOUM OF THE WITCH GIRL

(From "The Desrick on Yandro" by Manley Wade Wellman)

For you've gone away, gone to stay awhile—
But you'll come back, if you come ten thousand miles.

On Yandro's hill all lone
Here in my desrick cold
I sit as still as stone
Until the years be told.

Here in my desrick cold
Dead-to-the-world-alive,
Until the years be told:
Fourscore and ten and five.

Dead-to-the-world-alive,
My hatred here I nurse:
Fourscore and ten and five
The summing of the curse.

My hatred here I nurse
For one who stole my heart;
The summing of the curse
My work of witch's art.

For one who stole my heart
Its cry sounds: *"Look away . . ."*
My work of witch's art?
I'll toll him back someday.

Its cry sounds: *"Look away . . ."*
Because I am no wife;

I'll toll him back someday
When nests are filled with life.

Because I am no wife,
Slow, slow the seasons go;
When nests are filled with life
My womb is filled with snow.

Slow, slow the seasons go
Because he did me wrong:
My womb is filled with snow,
But lava is my song.

Because he did me wrong
I fill the hills with mist;
But lava is my song.
From lips too long unkissed.

I fill the hills with mist,
The wild beasts hear my words;
To lips too long unkissed
Fetch food like Bible birds.

The wild beasts hear my words—
Bammat and Flat and Skim—
Fetch food like Bible birds
Till one day they'll fetch—him.

Bammat and Flat and Skim,
Toller and Culverin,
Till one day they'll fetch him
Right to my door—and in.

Toller and Culverin
(All things must have their feed)
Right to my door—and in.
As earth must drink its seed,

All things must have their feed,
Whether the hawk or dove—
As earth must drink its seed,
The heart must draw its love.

Whether as hawk or dove,
I'll welcome him inside;
The heart must draw its love,
Denied—then satisfied.

I'll welcome him inside
Where I sit still as stone;
Denied—then satisfied
On Yandro's hill all lone.

PANTOUM OF THE WRAITH-KINGS

"A mortal, Frodo, who possesses one of the Great Rings
does not grow or obtain more more life; he merely continues,
until each day is a weariness."
–J.R.R. Tolkien, *THE FELLOWSHIP OF THE RING*

No circling golden rings,
The year for us unwound:
We Nine, the wizard-kings,
We lived our lives unbound;

The years for us unwound,
We loved and warred and wrought,
We lived our lives unbound,
But wider realms we sought.

We loved and warred and wrought,
We thought to die as men,
But wider realms we sought
Beyond the mortal ken.

We thought to die as men,
Yet life unending craved;
Beyond the mortal ken—
The very dream enslaved.

Yet life unending, craved,
Made true life fly the faster;
The very dream enslaved—
And slaves must have a master.

Made true life fly the faster,
Till One came from afar

(For slaves must have a master):
Men called him Annatar.

Till One came from afar,
Our days flowed like a river.
Men called him Annatar;
He was of gifts the giver.

Our days flowed like a river,
But, o, he bent their frame:
He was of gifts the giver
And Sauron was his name.

But, o, he bent their frame—
Woe to ambition blinding!
And Sauron was his name
Who shaped our doom of binding.

Woe to ambition blinding!
We thought our dream he aided,
Who shaped our doom of binding—
He drained us till we faded.

We thought our dream he aided—
None knew what did befall us;
He drained us till we faded,
And Ringwraiths now men call us.

None knew what did befall us.
We have the life desired:
And Ringwraiths now men call us,
Shadows in twilight 'tired.

We have the life desired?
Would he had never sought us!
Shadows in twilight 'tired,
Half-life that peddler brought us.

Would he had never sought us,
We Nine, the wizard-kings—
Half-life that peddler brought us
On circling golden rings.

PERFESSER ROSE AN' THE POET

In old age wandering on a trail of beauty, lively, may I walk.
–NAVAJO NIGHT CHANT

For Chuck "Wagon" Carter, Would-Be Poet "Lariat,"
On the Occasion of His Eightieth Birthday

Now you've likely heard tell of Eskimo Nell, or—if you've been readin' Service—
That "Lady Named Lou" who loved Dan McGrew, but don't you go gettin' nervous:
There's a woman weren't bawdy and weren't even haughty, fer all she was eddicated:
She wuz Perfesser Rose to her friends an' foes, an' any who asked, she aided.

This day it wuz two, an' one *wuz* a Lou, in the bunkhouse at Big Blue Welkin
(You know it—it's near the town o' Chawed Ear, the home o' Breckinridge Elkins.)
Well, t'other was Chuck, an' flat thunderstruck wuz Miz Rose when she come a-callin'
To find her friends at their pore wits' ends, an' Miz Lou's tears fast a-fallin.'

"They're a-cuttin' us loose, an' such abuse I never did think to suffer,
But the times is rough, and the new boss tough—reckon no horn toad is tougher.
I'm no good as a hand—can't rope, won't brand"—
                                        "Chuck, that ain't yer way o' givin."
No, he'd take his geetar an,' under the stars, he'd sing o' the lives they wuz livin.'

Then here come the boss, an' he looked as cross as a jes'-tail-trodden rattler,
An' he tipped his hat, but then he spat: "Ma'am, I've got no place fer a prattler.
"It may sound cold, but these folks is old—"
                                        "In body," snapped Rose, "not spirit!"
"Wal, I like Chuck an' Lou, an' the men do, too. If you've got a defense, I'll hear it.

"There's no place fer a bard when the work is hard an' the dogies sick or strayin'—
He's a sorry galoot with a horn to toot an' the 'brass' to want some payin'!
Now tell us, Miz Rose, why you suppose—cuz, if anyone knows, you'd know it—
Fer the camp or the trail or the hoosegow-jail, why we need a Cowboy Poet?"

Miz Rose, she grinned right down to her chin, an' laughed as she was li'ble,
Then she clapped her hands an' says to each man, "Now boys, get out yer Bibles!
'Man is not fed alone by bread'—that's Matthew Four-Four yer seekin'—
He knows bite an' sup, so you listen up—it's the BIG Camp Cook Who's speakin'!

"It wuz words, He said, were a soul's true bread, not other bait, He'd tell 'ee—
Cuz no barbecue-dish can be suffish, if the ache's not in the belly.
Now the desert is dry in deep July, an' nothin' ain't deader nor duller,
But under the rain it will bloom again, a heaven o' stars o' color!

The soul sleeps so, till it's called to grow, by song like a silvery river,
An' *somethin'* unfolds from the dark an' the cold, an' it knows it wuz delivered.
In their restin' or flyin' or livin' or dyin' the beasts must be dumb by nature,
But the makin' o' verse breaks our muteness-curse, for Man's the poetic 'craychur'!

"Take this man back in—what yer doin's a sin—an' if you wanna be smarter,
Ye'll serve all grub to the heart's *lub-dub*—in other words, 'a la Carter'!
Don't think of a wagon you'd hafta be draggin—yer Bard is a Chuck, there's no lyin'—
But his 'chuck' fer the soul is a watering-hole, with refreshment undryin,' undyin.'"

They hung their heads down till their snoots touched the
ground (well-nigh, they wuz so over-awed),
An' up come the cook, an' Chuck's hand he took, an'
"My pardner's a *Bardner!*" guffawed.

Then the couple he led to their old bunk-bed—
an,' as fer Miz Rose, she wuz listenin'—
Though she said nothin' more, when she turned from the
door, in her eyes happy tear-drops wuz glistenin.'

SCARECROW

(Based on the OUTER LIMITS Episode
"The Architects of Fear")

For My Brother Fred

If they draw your name
From the cosmic pot,
The uncommon one
From the common lot,

Know what to expect:
No world's applause,
But the clapping of mutated
Gibbonish paws.

They will stop your voice
And swap your breath
And warp you to Scene One,
Act Two, *Macbeth:*

Witches' hot-pot:
A possum-tail limb, a
Hen-foot, a head like a
Dream-Hiroshima.

A scarecrow will serve
To hurl birds from the grain,
But to guard the synapseeds
In furrows of brain

From the gore-crows of war
Wants "hard work, soft love"
To s'uncast the raven,
Unshadow the Dove.

The Mark Against Evil—
The Chrism of Christ—
Must be won by each one,
Self-sacrificed

In the fate of all scarecrows
Since capital He:
What falls from the sky
Must be hung on a Tree.

SKELETONS IN ARMOR

(From *BEDKNOBS and BROOMSTICKS*)

Have they not sworn, though dead, they would return
In Britain's hour of need, her warrior-horde?
Here, in this rusting-place of helm and sword,
Demand that price, good witch, or all will burn.
Call them with Wordsworth, conjure them from Donne:
    "England hath need of thee—arise, arise
    From Death, ye numberless infinities!"
Countless of body, true; in spirit, one.

Summon them now by that moon-magic spell
    Till Life's tide floods once more
    These shells on Death's dry shore;
Then, beyond hope, hear, see: the drumstick's knock
Like Conscience' knuckle on a soul's grimed pane;
The trumpets' throats washed clean by silver rain
Of martial cries; and, rising with the shock,
    A Pentecostal flame of pennoncel.

THE BAG LADY AT KING'S CROSS

I am the pilgrim,
Lame, but hunting the shrine.
            –Vachel Lindsay

Right at the station, here–
First o' September–
'Twixt Platforms Nine and Ten,
Eh, what I've seen!
Children and grownups, with
Things to be feared of,
Dressed in witch robes an' hats,
Like Hallowe'en!

Well, so I likes my gin?
Weather gets nippy!
But I stay dry while I
Watch what *they* do:
Just at eleven, they
Take their queer parcels,
Rush at the wall, an' then
Push themselves through!

Where do they journey to,
Eager an' shining?
(O, that bright girl, with the
Face like a star!)
Guess it's not always nice–
Must be some dangers–
(O, that poor boy, with the
Terrible scar!)

Reckon it's Faerie–no,
Pied Piper's mountain–
(*I* see the scarlet train,
I hear the call):
But I'm the crippled one,
Shut out for slowness–
O, if their *"All aboard"*
Only meant "all"!

THE BLACK GUARD'S BALLAD

IN MEMORY OF MITCHELL LEWIS

"Hail to Dorothy?"

I have beaten my sword to a plowshare
To cut but the flesh of the land,
And my halberd now harrows, not harries
The foes of my acres' span;
I have built me a home in the valley—
I have wedded, bred sons—all so right—
But I gaze, these bright years, to the mountains with tears
And remember my hour of Night.

I once served the Witch in her castle,
Captain of all her guard;
Black were the deeds that we did then,
Bleak was our life, and hard.
Most folk think we were unwilling slaves
(With the Tin Man, who rules us free),
But he knows naught of hearts, so new to that part,
As the Witch knew the heart of me.

When the moon rolls high like a crystal ball
In a sky like a wizard's gown,
I steal to the press where my uniform hangs
And tremblingly hale it down:
There is the coat of corpselight sheen
With trimmings as blood aflow;
The necklace of bone, and the busby's cone
Like a cloud of nightmare woe.

And these garments exhale an opiate fume
Till in vision I see once more

47

Our desperate charge, and the death-draught flung,
And our mistress a-twitch on the floor:
Now the sun stands above like Glinda's sphere
Before which all evils fall:
But, unshadowing Noon, I remember the moon—
And within me the Shadow stands tall.

THE CHRISTMAS PIRATE CHANTEY

(In Echo of Lindsay's "The Sea-Serpent Chantey")

"Somewhere there is a thief who has heard that people bury . . . their gold and jewels.
Can you see the expression on his face when he comes on what I have buried?"
–Joanne Greenberg, *I Never Promised You a Rose Garden*

Once I did find a shell
Cast by wind and tide;
Battered and black as hell
On the upper side;
But, when with foot of scorn,
That shell I overturned,
O, then was glory born—
For a rainbow burned!

Tell me, philosophers,
And wizard-men:
What lesson's written there
By no mortal pen?
If Nature so contrives
To bedeck these mindless things,
May not dull human lives
Hide the wealth of kings?

UnGuess'd to Come, our bark,
Under Meated Bones,
They fear who love the Dark
And must yet atone.
We right, by word and way,
The sin-inverted soul:
And bring to light of day
Its treasure-hold.

49

Our God's a man-o'-war,
And His stings He'll trail
Deeper to Man's sea-floor
Than the sounding whale;
What is His prey (o pray!)?
Each heart's perfected jewel—
That makes an Easter Day
And a pirate's Yule.

CHORUS:

We're Christmas Pirating—
And where'er we go,
No "Yo-ho-ho" we sing,
But "Yo-ho-ho-ho!"
Under the Berried Skull
The feast for all we spread:
Come, trusting as the gull
To the sailor's bread.

THE MANX

He wondered whether even the archangels understood the hornbill.
            —*G. K. Chesterton*

The God who made the hornbill
By tying on a bird
Behind a beak three times its size
Makes play through the Absurd

Creating crazy creatures;
And, once, He made a cat
Combining feline and lapine–
Compact, and so compat-

-ible, He must have thought them,
Or, "hoply," 'twas a frog;
But one thing's sure: the critter's no
More cat than it is dog.

This beast, the Manx, is fable
Who'd not give God the laud:
That those who will not mind may find
Their "tail" of days excaud-.

But, es-cat-ology aside
(Or, in its case, behind),
There's much to love about that cat:
A merry, loving mind,

A solemn, waddling toddle,
Deep, sweet tip-tilted eyes;
A curve to palm like pearl to shell
Of back's quick-quirked rise.

With Chesterton (and Hopkins,
Who also praised God's pranks),
Let us raise a Magnifi-Cat,
And for the Manx give—thanx.

THE OLD SAVOYARD, ON RE-READING THE LIBRETTO OF THE MIKADO

For Donald Adams

O Orient pearl of English minstrelsy!
Once more I greet you. Like a classic fan
You hold within your slow-unfolding span
A little world where Time has ceased to be.
A fan, indeed: upon a "cloth untrue,"
A few deft "characters" of old Japan;
And one may read the way of maid with man
In their Tit-Willow pattern ever new.

Yet is it but romance?
Mark here the canny satrap with his screed
Of exquisite chastisements itemized;
And there his son, that shrewd but youthful prince
Trembling on manhood's and on lordship's verge:
All lives and loves are tabled in his *lied,*
An Alexander's Feast, Nippon-devised.
Even so our days are song, as these evince,
Yin-Yang admixed, with laughter at the dirge,
Tears at the wedding dance!

L'ENVOI

THE PIRATE-POET to his MATE

Hail, Poetry, Heaven-born maid–
Thou gildest e'en the pirate's trade!
–W.S. Gilbert

When I have died, my friend, come walk the shore
At sunset, hour blood-gold, and think of me:
Should your eyes sting with salt not from the sea,
I'd be obliged. And then do two things more:
Send our ship, Viking-like, into the sun–
The fire this pyre-ate will but goldlier burn–
Bright, though a funeral-barge, from stem to stern,
Steered by a death-outgrinning skeleton!

Last, look to my book-quest: a modest [c]hoard
Of precious [s]tones; and, kneeling on the sand,
Pour forth the ditty-bag that was my heart:
Amethyst passions; rubied rabid screams;
Whims opal-changeful; starred black-sapphire dreams . . .
Less than the Goonies saved from Willy's hoard;
Some marbles Slightly lost in Neverland;
Out of a pirate's head, a poet's art.

54

THE SONG OF JAKE SULLY

(From *AVATAR)*

. . . to leave the world unseen
And with thee fade away into the forest dim.
–KEATS

All men are crippled coming here. The trip led me away from Earth,
With twisted legs and fisted mind, to find a wild and strange rebirth.
How could I guess, on gazing out, that hazy globe of azurite
Would hold the secret Terrans need, whose erring greed left Earth a blight?

Men came to scrape and rape this clod, though goddess-named it was: a chest
With treasures for the plundering, damn wondering and all the rest!
Curse Science for its tiptoe feet, blast Anthro for its kid-glove hands—
When Man the Plague departs, leave bleeding-hearts to find what Hope they can!

At first, I was the worst of all: the waterfall changed most of that.
In my Pandoran avatar, a startling blue-man tiger-cat,
I fell far, far from pride—not Grace—and then a Face looked into mine,
And though I did not know it then, I entered into the Divine.

Or did She enter into me? "I see you" were her simple words,
And yet the Seeing went so deep that Being's core itself I heard:
From floating stone to dragon-snake, to Make the Bond links every part—
This was what *we* lost, eons gone: our oneness with the Mother-heart!

Come with me on the forest way, and say the thing that Singers name:
A hammerhead-triceratops, its crest atop like Buddhist flame
May shatter by, or banshees rise, bright spatter-paintings taking flight,
Night-newts spin wheels of blushing flesh, and plushy moss will pulse with light,

Flaring and fading as we pass—alas that any sole should mar—
Only our souls should linger here, commingled with the Was and Are.
Now kneel beneath the Sacred Tree, that rosary with beads aglow,
Where SHE and all the Ancients throng, from the First Songs of long ago.

Just one more thing before I go: before, below, my name was Man:
"Jacob" who'd climb to God, but clod sin-sullied under Eden's ban.
"Silly" they call me, even now—how can it be, then, since the Fall,
I found the ladder to a heaven whose Mother has a place for all?

THE TASTER'S TESTAMENT

For Steven Vogel, M.D., (and fellow taster),
in honor of
"The sense of smell . . . God gave to us for ours."
–*G.K. Chesterton*

If one revealed he saw that wizard ray
Yet unDisclosed to men, hue octarine,
Or in our world heard the brain-needling keen
Piped by the pipistrelle to shape its way,
You might believe, and bid him speak and stay.
Then pray condemn not us, the indigenes
Of our strange supersensory demesne
(Demean not us, we plead:
'Tis "in the genes," indeed);
Where taste and smell hold sweet tyrannic sway.

We are the gourmand's truffle-snuffling swine,
Miner's canary, emperor's unicorn,
Guiding to bliss or giving tongue at bane.
We pity *you*, who are of "scents" forlorn–
And should we choose a Chestertonian line
To cry this cosmic wrong,
'Twould be from Quoodle's Song:
"They haven't got no noses!" the refrain.

THE TREE OF INNER WEATHER

Your head so much concerned with outer, mine with inner, weather.
–Robert Frost

For Sylvia Plath

My father held you once; he did not hold me;
That may be partly why I write. But still,
Sylvia, life is more than killing ill.
A Della Robbia cherub, Daddy told me,
You looked. I can see that. What I cannot see
(Speaking of angels) is why, unlike Blake,
Or any half-glassed optimist, you'd make
"Satan's men," not "seraphim," crowd every tree.

Speaking of trees, a cartoon by Gahan Wilson
Shows an artist painting a bare one he has swarmed
With *Things.* To a child who views the monstrous forms:
"I paint what I see," he says.
You whose verse fills un-
easels with witch-elms and your me, not you, tree:
When next you lift your dream-head from the ground,
May you grow like Yeats's laurel, poet crowned
With no Plathetic fallacy–a true tree.

THE TYRANT OF TERRATORRE

That tyrant . . . was Freedom's best and bravest friend.
–Byron

THE INCANTATION
Compunction, hence—Remorse, away—
The Dark must have its holiday—
Give me the face the mirrors flee—
Come, fiery Cup, and set me free!

Part First
. . . so complete in beauty and anger . . .
—Joanne Greenberg

Hot to the heart with wrath against the Wrong
(O, it will pay this time, my Enemy!),
I seek the Tower long hid within my mind
To seize the power all dread that I possess.
Shaking with rage—and trembling with desire—
I race the stair as secret as an ear
Clear to the storm-wreathed chamber. In a trice
The age-black door is slammed, the bolts shot home,
And I pause, panting, to survey the room:
Dim, damp, and shadowed, bare but for a plinth
And thereupon a goblet filled brimful.
All is prepared, for here *my* will is done!
Smiling with little mirth, I reach my hands
Forth to the massy vessel, lift it high
In blasphemous communion, and intone
The morphic rune incised about its base.
Wild thunder shakes the tower, and from above
A lance of lightning pierces through the roof
To smite the unholiest Grail, which bursts to flame.
Plunging my face within the sorcerous fire,

59

I gulp the contents: lurid, gelid, cold.
The potion crawls down, sliming like a snail,
Strikes bottom, torches, and I shriek aloud.
My body writhes and arcs, a gale-wrenched tree,
Then straightens as the longed-for change completes.
Now I stand tall, cadaverously thin,
Hair madman long and lank, hands vulture-clawed,
Mouth viper-lipless, nose a beak, and eyes
Lit by the flames that fume from Phlegethon.
Then one last gift the goblet grants me: garb
Dead black unbroken, boots and gown and cape
And iron-nailed gauntlets, sheathing half the arm.
On one forefinger glows a ruby clot
In curious setting, like a root half-gnawed—
Jack-o'-the-Lantern's coal that Satan gave
For light when Heaven and Hell had cast him out.
The transformation done, I seek the glass,
And, well pleased, pose and preen and stroke my robes;
But when I smile at this grim image, then
The quatrain's curse fulfills: the pane outwarps,
Inbuckles, smokes, and melts, to strike the flags
And seek their cracks in shivering silver beads.
I am amused: I have made something fear!
My poisoned blood intoxicates like wine,
And I throw back my head in pride of power
And laugh until the stones wince in the walls.

Part Second
. . . a creature of an older world maybe it was . . .
—J. R. R. Tolkien

Thence to the turret's roof, the task at hand.
The storm still rages, and its 'wildering winds
Send my cape streaming like the tempest-wrack;
And when I crook my steel-tipped talons high,
Exultingly, to call the lightnings down,
I find an anger worthy of my own.
The levin teased to tag my fingertips
Kindles the gloves in hand-of-glory flames
Wherewith I wash, like that false-gilded king
Of Serpent Mountain in Eternia.

My hands aglow with stol'n Promethean fire
I feel a god and, wanting worshipers,
Turn me to where my dwarfish servant Min
Now casts him prone upon the stony floor
(He has not far to fall, but the effect
Is gratifying to my swollen pride.)
"Hail, Lord!" he cries, arising, "would ye ride?
Moonshadow waits, but her impatience grows;
Best be a-faring, sir. Dark Wind—Wing—Way!"
He bows and vanishes, and where he stood
There ramps a beast that looks the Night-Mare's dam,
Bridling and sidling hard against her chain.
Bird beak, snake head, bat wings the creature wears;
Such was the steed that bore Lord Angore
And Angmar's Witch-king, of the Nazgul chief;
Shrowk, shantak, dragon, or pteranodon—
All these and none, but dractyl—mine alone!
Graciously, as one greets a hippogriff,
I bend my head (and even that nod comes hard),
With, "Living eclipse and troubler of men's dreams,
Minion and mate, Moonshadow, shall we fly?"
She kneels, assenting, and I mount, my seat
Above the membranous vanes, which now unfold;
A casual gesture, and her chain is naught—
Then with a step she lifts, and we are free!
Clearing the turret's lip in one great sweep,
She spirals upward in a "widening gyre"—
This falcon hears her falconer; we grow
One as a centaur. When we pass the moon,
Full, freshly washed, and brilliant with the hour,
We 'grave a hideous scrimshaw. Scrimshaw? Nay—
Say grimshaw—ha! My laugh bursts forth again,
Moonshadow answers with a cackling cry;
Then like a thunderclap she shuts her wings—
And down we plunge to reach the night's fell goal,
Arrowing earthward like a bolt of doom.

Part Third
"I do good—I do good—I do good!"
—W. S. Gilbert

61

You who have thought me evil by this tale—
Surprise! I have fooled you, and I do that well.
I am a Murgatroyd of Ruddigore,
Kentigern called, but nicknamed Mungo, "friend"—
One of that witch-damned race compelled to do
A crime a day or die in agony.
So nigh to Hatheg-Kla lies TerraTorre
That Chaos gnaws its shores incessantly;
For its defense, I needs must bless my curse:
Dark fortress, dread transforming, direful flight.
Each of my people keeps a votive-lamp,
An oratorre, in image of my tower,
By kindling which they summon me at need,
And any may, of whatso rank or age.
This night the call sounds from a garth far-flung
Ultramontane to Ulthar of the Cats,
And cats are all the tale (or tailless). "Help,
Sir, help!" –the speaker is a maid of ten—
"We had some kits born in our barn yestre'en;
They've got no tails, and Da says they are 'witched
And made me leave them to the Chaos-crawl;
But I crept back, and then the stuff came up,
And now I'm trapped and can't get out! Oh, please,
Save me, Lord Friend!" Well, such a pretty plea
Seldom has stroked my ears, and then I hate
Cruelty to little ones of beast or man.
Besides, I knew the nature of the kits
The girl defended; said I "beast or man"?
No, rather "beast of Man," for Manx they were,
Of all felines most ancient, brave, and wise.
Her boorish sire must have a lesson—and
Here comes the tutor now. A, B, C—cat!

Part Fourth
Lethe's mounting tide . . .
—Clark Ashton Smith

Cresting a final hill, we reached the farm—
Or what had been a farm until this night,
A fertile fan-out of the foothills, held
And held forth, like a maid's fruit-laden skirt.

Now, drowned in that vile slime, that eating gleet
Spewn from the ground when Chaos was aroused,
It seemed the Ring of Isengard despoiled,
A seething cauldron brimmed with hellish brew.
And in the midst a Cunning Mind, in truth:
My youthful summoner atop a shed,
One arm about a wicker frail, its mate
Frantically flagging. As we near the girl,
I see the Crawl snake up a tentacle
Seeking her foot, then touch it, loop it round—
"Down, child, and shield your eyes!" I cry; and swift-
Flinging me forward on the dractyl's neck,
I loose a bolt from out my fingertips
Straight to the slime-vine's root and slice it through.
Screaming, it curdles back, and I, too, scream
For joy of battle joined—my favorite fray!
Wheeling Moonshadow in a tight-reined arc,
I turn at the field's end, and now there rise
For one head hewn, a hundred Hydras more
Clamoring, clutching toward us—let them come!
Bracing my gauntlets on the wide-flung webs,
I murmur, "Now, sweet steed, receive my power—
And let wings beat'n to ploughshare and to sword
Mow this foul crop and make it feel my 'gilt'!"
Forth from my hands flows light, imMidasing
The bat-bird's vanes till each is edged with fire;
Then with a shout I spur her, and we dive,
Scything the stalking stalks like Death—nay, Life!
Down, round the garth we sweep and pass and turn,
Winnowing (ah, and may we but *win now!*).
The harvest done, we pass the 'leagured shed,
No Orthanc, but the narrowing isle of ash
In Orodruin's lava-vomit sea
Where small/great hearts so bravely waited doom.
No wraith's fell beast but Gwaihir-Windlord-like,
Moonshadow curls her talons round the girl
And those life-morsels cradled in the frail,
Then lifts them gently as a summer swing
And bears them to her house and our last hour.

Part Fifth

And for the Manx give—*thanx.*
—*Wolf*

Soon by a sturdy thatch-roofed croft we land;
Her cargo perilous and querulous,
The child hastes in, while I remain without,
Behind the door ajar. Her furious sire,
Waving a riding-crop for no horse meant
Rages into the room: "You wretched brat!
Grain lost, field blighted, and that *Thing* called out—
All for some stunted cats! I'll drown them now!"
The furious farmer reaches for the frail,
His daughter blocks his path—he lifts his whip—
But the blow never falls, for stock and lash
Burst into flame at one last bolt I hurl.
"Bad night for 'crops,'" I comment, stepping in.
"Still here, old horror?"
"Father, he's our friend!"
"And shall be, till both 'brat' and cats are safe.
Now for the purrpetrators of your crimes."
The basket's lid is lifted, and behold,
One anxious mother Manx and four fine young,
Murmurous and milky, nestled by her side.
"These you would kill? I think not." Then a tale
Less of their ancient lineage, wit, and strength
I tell, than of their deadly skill with rats.
That wins him, and he kneels to kiss my ring,
Promising tribute of the litter's best.
"Heed Gandalf's words," I warn him at the door,
"In this as all things: do not be in haste
To deal out death till you have seen all ends.
You have seen five and—wise man! —bade them live;
Cherish all life, but most this plucky child,
And so be foe to Chaos. Now farewell."

Epilogue
The revel that ends too soon . . .
—*W.S. Gilbert*

Thence to Moonshadow. Towerwards we wend,
A nightmare nigh asleep upon the wing,

And we are home in moments. Lighting down,
I cast my reins to Min and stroke my steed;
They vanish, and I am—myself? Not so,
But all the Mungo sunlit worlds can bear.
As I descend, the Torre unwinds behind
Till, when I reach its base, the shrunken spire
Rises roof-high, no higher. I, too, am less,
And now must face the mourning of the damned
Whose sabbats cease at cockcrow. Speed the eve
Ill and its infiltrations call once more:
Then—for the Right—the flight, the fight—*the night!*

THERESA AND TRELANE

(From the Classic Star Trek Episode
THE SQUIRE OF GOTHOS)

For William Campbell

Pray tell me, lady, what it is you do
Wandering beneath the moon without a swain?
"Come live and be my love!"—the name's Trelane,
General, and squire, too;
The music plays, and we shall trip amain
A *pas-de-deux*.

Or pas-de-*Dieux*—I like *that* spelling more!
Beware boy-gods, Therese—myself, to start,
Dan Cupid next, who with heart-headed dart
Can wound full sore;
We, beau-men both, have in the archer's art
A perfect score.

Rings for your fingers! Music where you go!
All lovers promise worlds, but which have proved?
Them you who years have far- and star-ward roved
Have seen, and thus you know
I only, of all men who ever loved,
Can make it so.

While stars in sarabande move, lord and dame,
What cheer, my sweet! Then make a little stay,
And join the dance, and fear no more than they
For name and fame;
Till daybreak, "when the shadows flee away,"
Come play the game!

THREE BALLOONS

(Seen But Not Snagged, Except Metaphorically,
From the Porch of a Restaurant in Orlando, Florida)

Once, on an awful noon,
Three balloons came as boon
(Loosed from a bride's festoon,
I am supposing);
A festive restive row
Under the portico,
Urging each other, *"Go!"*
Nuzzling and nosing.

One pinky-piggy-clean,
Two cool in minty green—
Three pearls of moony sheen
Ribbon-tails trailing;
Just as I came anear,
Signal was given clear
(I swear I heard a cheer)—
Off they went sailing!

Like Darling children's flight
Pan-danced through nightied-night
"Second star to the right,
Straight on till morning,"
Wish-like they were in rise—
Souls sprung to holy skies,
All calls of Earth, all cries
Of love or warning.

On to the moon, or higher,
They flew as men aspire
Bubbles of air and fire
Heavenward ascending;
That was *our* wedding day:
Moon-egg meets tossed bouquet,
Astroseeds cast her way,
Earth and space blending!

TO JAFAR, TRANSFORMED INTO A GENIE

"Infinite power—very small living space."
—ALADDIN

Having gotten the immortal gift, do you deem it worth all?
Billow higher than Allah, exulting, and never refrain you!
But look not down, lest you glimpse on our puny Earth-ball
The Clamps and the Lamp awaiting you, fain to restrain you.

TRIOLET: TREE TO LET

If women were trees, the merely fair
As willows graceful-green would grow,
But weep at birds' nests in their hair—
If women were trees. The merely fair
Would grow so. Better spread to air
Wide arms to 'brace birds, boys; below,
Open the heart to nest and lair.
If women were trees, the merely fair
As willows graceful-green would grow.

TRON'S HYMN

I'll take his hand and go with him
To the deep wells of light;
As unto a stream we will step down
And bathe there in God's sight.
            –Dante Gabriel Rossetti

ENCOmium I bring, Logos, my One:
Behold, in souled state, Tron looking up:
Drop down, I pray you, dew, that I may sup
Your light: by nary other food I run.
Praise I upraise, cup-raise! The sky's blue screen
Disparities no more made-man, man-made,
Since one impulsive godling earthed mis-ley'ed
And the Unseen Clued in among the Seen.

Yet though, while current here,
He bore a touch resolved to life again
The very dead, still what in him was slight
My memory guards most dear:
A bit he walked in usage friendly-wise
With us, empowered our equals.
            "Through such men,
God, stooping, shows sufficient of His light
For us in the dark to rise by. And I rise."

WHITE SANDYLION

"Thuh—thuh—thuh—that's all, folks!"
          –*Porky Pig*

Rush-shroom of star-stuff—
Self-breeze-blown dandelion—
Your name is A-bomb.

A
MINI
CINEMA
SONGBOOK :

LYRICS FOR THEMES
FROM SIX FAVORITE
FANTASY FILMS

HOGWARTS FOREVER!

(The Wizarding School Anthem from
HARRY POTTER and the SORCERER'S STONE)

Hail, ancient school, seat of magic lore and learning—
Bastion of power and beacon of light!
Once more to thee we come joyfully returning;
So, ceasing never,
Praising thee ever,
HOGWARTS FOREVER!
We sing tonight.

SEEK THE LIGHT

(Main Title Theme from *TRON)*

"Every tower is lighting up!"
  –Arc-keeper Dumont

Seek the light
Glowing high in heaven;
Seek the light
Flowing from above:
Ill may vanquish me—
Still my cry shall be:
"Seek the light of Kevin—
Seek the light of Love!"
Find the light
Dimming suns as levin;
Find the light
Brimming holy wells;
Let no prayers uprise—
Yet I quest the skies:
Find t he Light where Kevin dwells!

SPACED-OUT RHYTHM

(Cantina Band Music from *STAR WARS*)

You will never find a more wretched hive of scum and villainy.
—*Obi-Wan Kenobi*

Strollin' down a dusty street
Far away and long ago,
Spaced-out rhythm caught my feet
And it wouldn't let me go—
Traced it to a spacemen's bar
On the tough side of the town;
Heard the song,
And hummed along,
And then I wrote it down:

"Woe, Mos!
Woe, Mos!
You're a wicked city!
Oh, Mos—
Oh, Mos—
(But your girls are pretty);
So, Mos—
So, Mos—
Gonna sing your ditty:

Women and wine from a thousand suns
For a thousand nights and one!"

THE JEDI ANTHEM

(Main Title Theme from *STAR WARS*)

Come, ye Knights of the Jedi—
Glorious our vision,
Holy our quest!
Hence, and take up the battle—
We may not falter,
Nor may we rest!

With the Sword of Power to be as a burning brand,
We shall light the way to Liberty:
Let us strive to serve the Right on sky and sea and land,
Never ceasing till all peoples shall be free!

Go, the Force will be with us—
Ever to guide, to
Strengthen and bless!
Forth, for Justice and Mercy—
Right to reward, and
Wrong to redress!

Pilgrim-guides are we to travelers gone astray
In the desert waste of Sin and Night:
May we turn their feet in to a green and healing way
That will lead them to the wells of living Light!

THE MAGIC CALL

*(Main Title Theme from HARRY POTTER
and the SORCERER's STONE)*

Though Time has been long in turning,
The hour has struck at last:
The children, the child,
The wise, the wild
Have come to redeem the past!

CHORUS:

*Away—away—o come away—
Your destiny—hear it call!
Obey—obey—make no delay—
The world is in Darkness' thrall.*

If any say, "No returning—
The time of the Great has died;
Long past is the age
Of knight and mage—"
I tell you that man has lied!

CHORUS:

*'Tis you—'tis you—this deed must do—
None else can work Evil's woe:
Be true—be true—to all renew:
So rise at the call—and go.*

THRONE-ROOM MARCH

(Finale from *STAR WARS)*

Lo, the conquering heroes come
From the war that set the star-men free:
They have quenched the lightning which had sundered a world,
By the Force of Life they vanquished—
Hail their victory!

With the Sword of Power to be as a burning brand,
We shall light the way to Liberty:
Let us strive to serve the Right on sky and sea and land,
Never ceasing till all peoples shall be free!

Lo, the conquering heroes come
Let us bend the head and bow the knee:
By the Force they vanquished—let all men give them hail,
And rejoice—even so shall we!

Printed in the United States
by Baker & Taylor Publisher Services